Stop That Ball

Alan MacDonald

Illustrated by
Doffy Wier

OXFORD
UNIVERSITY PRESS

Jess liked football. A football coach came to her school.

He picked her to be a
ball-girl.

Jess went to the match. Her job was to fetch the ball.

The match began. The ball
went out. Jess was fast. She
got to the ball first.

Then the ball went over the goal...

...out of the ground!

Jess ran out of the ground. She looked for the ball.

The ball was on a truck. Jess ran after it.

The truck stopped. She saw the ball.

Jess asked the workman for the ball.

A workman got the ball. He dropped it to Jess.

Can you throw it back, please?

11

But a dog got it first! Jess ran after the dog.

The dog jumped in a puddle.

Jess got the ball at last. It was very wet.

She got back to the ground. But the match was over!

The coach let Jess keep the ball.
All the team signed it.